Franziska Schweitzer

Peter Pan Reimagined

A Comparison of Brom's *The Child Thief* and J. M. Barrie's *Peter Pan*

Anchor Academic
Publishing

Schweitzer, Franziska: Peter Pan Reimagined. A Comparison of Brom's *The Child Thief* and J. M. Barrie's *Peter Pan*, Hamburg, Anchor Academic Publishing 2016

Buch-ISBN: 978-3-96067-012-4
PDF-eBook-ISBN: 978-3-96067-512-9
Druck/Herstellung: Anchor Academic Publishing, Hamburg, 2016
Covermotiv: © Franziska Schweitzer

Bibliografische Information der Deutschen Nationalbibliothek:
Die Deutsche Nationalbibliothek verzeichnet diese Publikation in der Deutschen Nationalbibliografie; detaillierte bibliografische Daten sind im Internet über http://dnb.d-nb.de abrufbar.

Bibliographical Information of the German National Library:
The German National Library lists this publication in the German National Bibliography. Detailed bibliographic data can be found at: http://dnb.d-nb.de

All rights reserved. This publication may not be reproduced, stored in a retrieval system or transmitted, in any form or by any means, electronic, mechanical, photocopying, recording or otherwise, without the prior permission of the publishers.

Das Werk einschließlich aller seiner Teile ist urheberrechtlich geschützt. Jede Verwertung außerhalb der Grenzen des Urheberrechtsgesetzes ist ohne Zustimmung des Verlages unzulässig und strafbar. Dies gilt insbesondere für Vervielfältigungen, Übersetzungen, Mikroverfilmungen und die Einspeicherung und Bearbeitung in elektronischen Systemen.

Die Wiedergabe von Gebrauchsnamen, Handelsnamen, Warenbezeichnungen usw. in diesem Werk berechtigt auch ohne besondere Kennzeichnung nicht zu der Annahme, dass solche Namen im Sinne der Warenzeichen- und Markenschutz-Gesetzgebung als frei zu betrachten wären und daher von jedermann benutzt werden dürften.

Die Informationen in diesem Werk wurden mit Sorgfalt erarbeitet. Dennoch können Fehler nicht vollständig ausgeschlossen werden und die Diplomica Verlag GmbH, die Autoren oder Übersetzer übernehmen keine juristische Verantwortung oder irgendeine Haftung für evtl. verbliebene fehlerhafte Angaben und deren Folgen.

Alle Rechte vorbehalten

© Anchor Academic Publishing, Imprint der Diplomica Verlag GmbH
Hermannstal 119k, 22119 Hamburg
http://www.diplomica-verlag.de, Hamburg 2016
Printed in Germany

Table of contents

1. Introduction 3
2. The Neverland 5
    2.1. Barrie's Neverland 5
    2.2. Brom's Avalon 7
3. The Characters 11
    3.1. Peter Pan 11
    3.2. Cernunnos, the Horned One 18
    3.3. The Females in Peter's Life 20
        3.3.1. Wendy, Tinker Bell and Tiger Lily 20
        3.3.2. Sekeu – Warlord or Mother? 24
        3.3.3. Modron 28
    3.4. The Lost Boys 31
        3.4.1. Barrie's Lost Boys 31
        3.4.2. Brom's Lost Children 32
    3.5. The Pirates 35
        3.5.1. Barrie's Pirates 35
        3.5.2. Brom's Settlers 37
4. Conclusion 40
5. Bibliography 42

1. Introduction

James Matthew Barrie was born 1860 in Scotland. When he was still a boy, his older brother died (cf. Birkin 5[1]) and it seems that Barrie has drawn some of his inspiration from this boy, who would never grow old (cf. B. 5). Barrie started his writing career during his time at Dumfries Academy with the play *Bandalero the Bandit* (cf. B. 2, 9). His marriage with Mary remained childless (cf. B. 35), and he found his substitute children in George, Jack, Peter, Michael and Nicholas – Arthur and Sylvia Llewelyn Davies' sons – for whom he wrote *Peter Pan*. Peter Pan first appeared in the *Little White Bird*, which "follows his relationship with George" (B. 57). Barrie wrote about George something that is in a way the personification of Peter Pan and vice versa: "There never was a cockier boy" (B. 42, P.P. 27). According to Lesnik-Oberstein, Barrie acted smartly by portraying George. She states that a child wants to read about children who are alike to the reading child (cf. Lesnik-Oberstein 225). Writers like Barrie "adjured children to be 'childlike' – to repudiate adult values in favour of fantasy, play and joyous anarchy" (Wood 159).While there is no indication that the relationship of Barrie and the boys ever exceeded the socially acceptable bonds between adult men and boys, it happened during a time, in which "many others violated or contemplated violating the boundaries our culture has placed between children and adult sexualities" (qtd. in Wood 156). After their father's death in 1907 (cf. B. 153) and Sylvia's death in 1910 (cf. B. 193), Barrie adopted the five boys (cf. B. 244). George's death during the First World War and Michael's drowning in the Sandford Pool left Barrie heartbroken and considering suicide (cf. B. 292, 294). While Barrie seemed shy, reserved or even a bit unsociable to adult people, children had a completely different view on him.

> To him [George] he was […] a small man with a cough who could wiggle his ears and perform magic feats with his eyebrows. Moreover he seemed to be singularly well-informed on the subject of cricket, fairies, murders, pirates, hangings, desert islands and

---

[1] Due to the high frequency with which I will be quoting Andrew Birkin, Barrie's *Peter Pan* and Brom's *The Child Thief*, I will from now use for parenthetical quotations from Andrew Birkin's book *J M Barrie and the Lost Boys* a capital B., for quotations from *Peter Pan* a P.P. and for quotations from *The Child Thief* a C.T.

verbs that take the dative. George had never met anyone quite like him; he was old, but he was not grown up. He was one of them. His unpredictable moods made him all the more intriguing. Some days he would be in the giving vein, and could be relied upon to tell an endless supply of stories, while at other times he would be steeped in silence. These silences, [...] were accepted by George as an integral part of his character. (B. 41)

Barrie gloried in the boys' waywardness, was George's companion and therefore no outsider (cf. B. 61). He even alluded to himself as Peter Pan in using the Davies family as basis for the Darling family in *Peter Pan* (cf. B. 61-64).Though Barrie loved playing with children, Shaw doubts that Barrie had ever been a child, "for the essential Barrie was a Puckish fairy – very whimsical, very playful, but ancient and [...] sad" (Shaw 153).

Though Barrie and Brom both stem from modest, middle-class families, their cultural backgrounds differ greatly. Since Barrie's time our society has undergone major changes. While Barrie grew up in a world prior to the invention of modern media, Brom was born in Georgia, USA, in 1965 (cf. imdb.com *Brom*) and grew up on army bases in many different countries, such as Japan, Hawaii and Germany (cf. bromart.com/bio). Contrary to Barrie, he grew up with music from records and movies that featured animated monsters. *The Child Thief*, therefore, was written in a cultural setting that differs greatly from Barrie's background. Nonetheless does the book stand in the tradition of the urban Gothic novel, since the urban setting and the sublime, magical world entwine and become one, as Peter Pan walks easily between the worlds in and brings his ancient, dark, magical kingdom into the New York of today where it causes mayhem. It mirrors the problems of society of today; Children's abuse, brutality, armed robbers and street gangs, which have a greater political and social impact today than during Barrie's time. In *The Child Thief* we encounter two different time frames, past and present, and different points of view. Barrie on the other hand used only a single time frame with a linear story line and one third-person narrator. This poses the question, which traits of the original *Peter Pan* Brom used, which ones he twisted, and which parts of the story he invented for the sake of a greater appeal to his readers.

2. The Neverland

Barrie's Neverland and Brom's Avalon show some similar traits and some differences. They are treated in the following part of this paper in order to evaluate the impact of their differences on the storyline.

2.1. Barrie's Neverland

The Neverlands or the Neverland was born out of the many stories that Barrie invented for Llewelyn Davies' five sons. It is a place where you go in your dreams and fantasies, a place that is not within our reality. The island is described as "always more or less an island, with astonishing splashes of colour here and there, and coral reefs and rakish-looking craft in the offing, and savages and lonely lairs, and gnomes who are mostly tailors" (P.P. 6). When the Darling children arrive on Neverland together with Peter Pan for the first time, they see the lagoon, turtles burying their eggs, a cave, a wolf with her whelps and the boat which belongs to Michael (cf. P.P. 43). The Neverlands consist of children's dreams and wishes. That is why "the Neverlands vary a good deal" (P.P. 7). They are also often very obscure and abstruse: "John's, for instance, had a lagoon with flamingos flying over it [...] while Michael [...] had a flamingo with lagoons flying over it" (P.P. 7). This is proof that the Neverland is shaped by the children's imagination.

It seems that within the Neverlands there is an island which is called Neverland. As imaginary as the Neverland is, it can become very real, especially within the two minutes before one goes to sleep (cf. P.P. 7). This Neverland is portrayed as an exciting place, alluring and tempting, but it is also a place full of dangers, and when the evening comes and the night sets, then the dreams and fantasies of adventurous quests become frightening and threatening: "then unexplored patches arose in it and spread; black shadows moved about in them; the roar of the beasts of prey was quite different now, and above all, you lost the certainty that you would win" (P.P. 44). The Neverland which is portrayed in *Peter Pan* seems to be often warm enough for the Lost Boys to bathe in the lagoon and lie in the sun on Marooners' Rock (cf. P.P. 86-87), yet it must also be occasionally cold enough for snow to fall (cf. P.P. 138). Barrie writes about the Neverland: "Of all delectable islands the Neverland is the snuggest and most compact; not large and sprawly, you know, with tedious distance between one adventure and another, but nicely crammed" (P.P. 7). Time and space seem to be of little consequence on this island, for once it is described as "most compact" (P.P. 7), but, then again, it has to be big enough for the Lost Boys, the Pirates, the Red-skins and the beasts of prey to miss each other when searching for one another (cf. P.P. 52). In one scene the wildlife of the Neverland is described a bit more closely, especially the dangerous side of the fauna: "lions, tigers, bears, and the innumerable smaller savage things [...]. Their tongues are hanging out, they are hungry to-night" (P.P. 56). The gigantic crocodile is also mentioned there (cf. P.P. 56). Concerning the food on the island, we learn, that "their chief food was roasted breadfruit, yams, coconuts, baked pig, mammee-apples, tappa rolls and bananas, washed down with calabashes of poe-poe" (P.P. 78). Park Williams took a closer look at the food and found it to be a nearly exact duplicate of the food mentioned in the book *Typee* by Melville (cf. 483). But Barrie seems to have mistaken the tappa rolls for food, instead of understanding them as the "kind of cloth made from fiber" which they are (Park Williams 483).

The Neverland is not only a place of make-believe, reality and adventure, it is also a place with a connection to the ever-after, the realm of the dead. Peter Pan, who whisks away the Darling children, can be read as death – as I will explain later in the Peter Pan section – and his realm (cf. Hunter 69-70), the Neverland, as the afterlife. Barrie writes that "when children died he [Peter Pan] went part of the way with them, so that they should not be frightened" (P.P. 8). The ancient Greeks believed that going to sleep was alike to dying (cf. Evslin 10), for the god of death, Thanatos, was the twin of Hypnos, the god of sleep (cf. theoi.com/Thanatos, theoi.com/Hypnos). They were the sons of the goddess Nyx, who incorporated the night (cf. H. Rose 20). The Darling children do not vanish during daytime – they vanish after their night-lights go out. Wendy explains to her mother, that Peter visits her at night, sits on the foot of her bed and plays on his pipes to her. But she "unfortunately never woke" (P.P. 9). In this scene, the link between the Neverland and the land of dreams is strong. Peter Pan comes from the Neverland and resides in Wendy's dreams, but at some point Peter Pan steps out of the dreamland and becomes real, and with him the Neverland. Of the night, after Wendy talked to her mother about Peter, Barrie writes the following: "She [Wendy] dreamt that the Neverland had come too near and that a strange boy had broken through from it" (P.P. 10). This means that this Neverland is not only occupying imaginary space, but also actual space, and that it can move. It seems that the more one loses oneself within one's dreams, the nearer does the Neverland come. The Neverland Barrie created became real for him and the five Davies children by enacting pirate or other adventure stories and generally imagining themselves within this realm of fairy. Barrie turned his adventures with the boys at the Black Lake during the summer holidays into "profitable account as further material for *The Little White Bird*" (B. 92). Thus the Neverland is partly fiction and partly real, when it is enacted during play and comes to life. It is also the home of dreams and adventures you could not have while being awake.

2.2. Brom's Avalon

Our modern times see a revival of the old beliefs, such as Àsatru or Wiccan. Brom is picking up on this New Age wave and uses Ynis Avallach, Avalon, as the Neverland, which is, as we will see, in many ways a sensible choice. But before analysing the Avalon in *The Child Thief*, we need the background lore on which Brom built his Avalon in order to compare the Brom's Avalon with its origins.

Avalon was named after the god Avallach, Afallach, or Avalloc – depending on whether one derives the name from Welsh *afal*, Cornish and Breton *aval* or from the Old Irish *abhall* (cf. Krappe 303). Avallach's name is connected to a fruit, the apple, because the island that was named after him had a strong connection to this fruit. "The Celtic texts definitely associate Avallon and [...] Avallach with apples" (Krappe 318). The apple can be interpreted as a symbol for and a fruit of immortality and youth (cf. Krappe 317). In addition, the apple is a fruit said to be "growing in a far-off land described as a paradise" (Krappe 317). The fact that Avalon is far away can mean two things: Firstly, that it was believed far away in space and therefore unreachable, and secondly, that it was far away in time insofar as it was the realm of the afterlife. Concerning the second way of reading Avalon, Krappe states that Avalloc was the Celtic god of death and that "if Avallo or Avallach is a chthonian, i.e. king and ruler over the dead, his kingdom, [...] is necessarily the abode of the departed, i.e. a *Toteninsel*" (314). The apple still fits the realm of the dead as a symbol, since it was a symbol for immortality, and while the gods are immortal, the dead cannot die again. In the Arthurian tale, King Arthur is brought to Avalon after his death by Morgaine La Fey (cf. Peyton III 59, 62).

This leads us to the mythical figure of Morgaine La Fey, who has her origin in Modron. Morgaine "inherited the family relationships and the role of Modron" (Loomis *Morgain* 200), which in turn leads us back to Brom's depiction of the Neverland in the form of Avalon. He inserted a section at the end of the book, where he lists the source ideas he used for his creation of Avalon (cf. C.T. 479), sadly Brom does not list them with a bibliography, but simply retells, what he has found in unknown source texts. Brom states that

> Avalon is closely associated with a similar Otherworld island, Tír na nÓg, called in English the *Land of Eternal Youth* or the *Land of the Ever Young* and thus I combined both mystical islands to some degree. Tír na nÓg [...] was where the Tuatha de Dé Danann, or Sidhe, settled when they left Irelands surface. Tír na nÓg was considered a place beyond the edges of the map, located far to the west. [...] Tír na nÓg is a place where sickness and death do not exist. It is a place of eternal youth and beauty. (C.T. 480-481)

Marie-Louise Sjoestedt contradicts Brom's findings insofar, as she states that "the *Tuatha* 'returned underground' where they continue to live in those mounds where the peasant of today still believes them to dwell" (13). According to Sjoestedt, time and space in Tír na nÓc (spelling cf. Sjoestedt 48) differ from our measures. "By entering their [Sídhe, Tuatha] world, humans leave human measures behind" (Sjoestedt 50-51), which can have fatal consequences; There are many stories about humans venturing into the land of faery, dancing the night away with the magical creatures, and re-emerging a lifetime older. Early poets described Tír na nÓc as "rich in fruits and flowers, men and women eternally young and divinely beautiful" (Sjoestedt 48), but the description of the Lands of Youth depended on whether the Sidhe or Tuatha de Danann acted as hosts or as enemies. They could be either dangerous to the Sons of Míl, the forefathers of the Irish, or generous hosts to the Irish heroes (cf. Sjoestedt 49). Due to the different flow of time in our world and the world of the Sidhe, only during the night of Samhain could humans enter and leave the other world unscathed, because in this night the "eternity of the *Sid* pierces through the time and suspends it temporarily" (transl., orig. emphasis Le Roux 39). The night of Samhain, which denotes the Celtic New Year, "belongs neither to one year, nor the other, and is, as it were, free from temporal restraint" (Sjoestedt 52).

On this night the two races can meet – either as friends or as enemies (cf. Sjoestedt 54, 56). Time flows differently in the Land of Youth, if it flows at all: "These folk of the Síd [...] do not differ much from men except in one respect. Being eternally young, they are" (Sjoestedt 50). Brom incorporated this feature into his book (cf. C.T. 97).

According to Brom's Peter Pan, Avalon is "a secret place. An enchanted island. No grown-ups allowed. It's full of faeries, goblins, and trolls [...]. We play with spears and swords and sometimes [...] we fight *monsters*" (orig. emphasis C.T. 24). At the age of six, Peter comes to Avalon on his own accord. He enters Avalon through a ring of stones, which could be an allusion to Stonehenge. Three ghostly girls tell Peter that he could come, if he really wished for it (cf. C.T. 133). In Avalon he meets a witch named Ginny Greenteeth (cf. C.T. 125), elves (cf. C.T. 143), and, most importantly, Ginny's sister: "the Lady Modron, daughter of Avallach", "the Lady of the Lake and the Queen of all Avalon" (C.T. 142). After Peter becomes her son, he sees a whole garden full of life and faeries of many different kinds (cf. C.T. 175). He gets to know Avalon as an island teeming with magic, life and laughter, except for Ulfger, who seems to be the exception to the rule (cf. C.T. 176). At that time, Avalon was full of magic that resided in everything, with the Lady of the Lake and the tree of Avallach as its heart. This former paradise is now threatened by the Flesh-eaters, who have become corrupted by Avalon's magic because "they have lost their magic to the fear and hatred they harbour for all that they can't explain, control, or understand. And so the magic twists them" (C.T. 254). The troll Tanngnost tells the whole story of what has happened to Avalon:

> Before forever ago, the very earth itself was alive, a place of mystery, nature and magic. It was the time of the first races, when gods still walked among us and we rejoiced in their miracles and wonderment. Men-kind shared this world for but a blink, then, sadly, they became enlightened, found science and religion. [...] Earth's first children were driven into the shadows by flame and cold iron, by man's insatiable need of conquest. Those who could escape Men-kind's persecution gathered around [...] Modron [...]. She released the Mist to hide and guard Avalon, and the isle became a refuge, a sanctuary from the human world. (C.T. 248)

The island began to drift away from "the Britains, drifting for an age along the frozen coasts of the Atlantic, until finally finding a home in the land now known as the Americas" (C.T. 249). This happened before the first settlers came and when the land was still "wild and full of magic" (C.T. 249). Even Abraham, one of the Lost Children, remembers a time, when Avalon was nearly healthy, when "these forests were lush, teeming with life. Every kind of fruits and nuts you could imagine. Why there were wild bananas hanging of the trees… a true paradise" (C.T. 163). When Avalon docked onto North America, the Lady called the Mist back into the lake and everything seemed to be fine. But eventually the European settlers came, not knowing that they had landed on Avalon instead of on the American mainland. The Lady sent out a "fellowship representing many of the faerie folk" which was slaughtered by the settlers, and thus the war for Avalon began (C.T. 250). This war, that continues up to the book's present, is not only a war between newcomers and an indigenous population, it is also a war between two religions – one embracing everything that is alive without judging anyone according to his looks, the other one restrictive and conquering –, and it is a war between nature and domestic life. After the first onslaught of the settlers, Avalon still was the very heart of faery, but it had become fragile. The Lady of the Lake withdrew in sorrow, shrouding the island again in mist, stopping other settlers from arriving, but also unintentionally trapping the settlers on the island. The magic that keeps Peter and the children young and alive for centuries (cf. C.T. 97, 254) corrupts the grown-up settlers. Tanngnost thinks that the Mist does more than hide Avalon. He thinks that it takes them, the fairies and Avalon, to a different time and place, which would explain why "time moves to much slower" on the island (C.T. 257). The magic of Avalon, though fading, still resides within everything, especially within the food made out of the plants that grow there and which the Devils, Brom's lost children, eat. Danny explains it in the following way: "Sekeu told me the magic's in everything here: the air, the water. When you eat it, though, you're ingesting it directly. This gunk […] is mostly made up of acorns. But like everything around here, there's magic in them […] like magical steroids" (C.T. 120-121). This kind of magic differs from the kind of magic Barrie describes in *Peter Pan*. Avalon's magic is not made out of dreams and wishes, it is an older kind of magic, a magic rooted within the soil. Tanngnost says that Brom's Avalon is a unity of many living beings: "The Tree is the heart, Avalon is the body, the inhabitants the soul, all three woven together, one living entity. One cannot be without the other" (C.T. 249).

3. The Characters

The characters of Barrie's *Peter Pan* were Brom's source for creating his own set of characters. This brought on interesting changes in the characters' relationships and their influence on each other.

3.1. Peter Pan

Peter Pan is a complicated, multi-faceted and difficult character to understand. Due to this, the approach to Peter's person must differ from the approaches to the other persons and instances. The crucial point to Peter is his history. That is why the approach to Peter will be linear and not split between *Peter Pan* and *The Child Thief*[2].

"According to Barrie, all children were birds once" (B. 62) and could fly. This includes Peter Pan. While stranded on an island, he meets Solomon, a wise bird. Peter still believes that he can fly, but Solomon tells him that he is "half-and-half" (B. 65) and will never again be able to fly. In *Peter Pan*, Peter tells Wendy that he ran away the day he was born because he heard his mother and father talk about him growing up, which he never wanted to do (cf. P.P. 28). Peter then stays with the fairies, who teach him how to fly without wings, and "now and again he flies home to watch his mother weeping for her lost child" (B. 64). However, when he finally decides to return to his mother for good, he cannot enter, due to the iron bars that she has put up in front of the window, and Peter has to witness her lying asleep "with her arm round another little boy" (B. 64). Brom calls this "just the sort of traumatic event to leave anyone a bit maladjusted" (bromart.com/childthief). When Peter sees the Darling children with their mother, Barrie writes that Peter "was looking through the window at the one joy from which be [sic] must be forever barred" (P.P. 171)

Unlike Barrie's human Peter Pan, whose story is tied to the Serpentine in Kensington Gardens and thus to Barrie's time (cf. B. 63), Peter Pan II starts his life as a changeling, or rather a half-breed, about 1400 years ago (cf. C.T. 56). Peter II is born to a family in Great Britain and at first accepted as a human child (cf. C.T. 58). Yet, when he climbs out of his basket, starts walking across the floor and then finally speaks to his

---

[2] In order to distinguish both Peters from each other, I will name Brom's Peter Peter II or Peter Pan II in this part.

family, he is instantly marked and feared as a changeling by the old woman (cf. C.T. 59). His mother tries to defend him, correctly explaining that "the one from the woods" – meaning Cernunnos – had taken her (C.T. 59), but no one listens. Out of fear, which turns into hatred, Peter II is thrown out of the house, and no amount of pleading changes Peter II's fate (cf. C.T. 60). According to folk lore, Peter II's treatment as a changeling is not unusual. Briggs lists a story in which the changeling is thrown into the fire, thus banished, and the original child is returned to its mother (cf. Briggs Position 6,194 of 33,383). Usually a changeling has to be tricked to show its real age and give away "his maturity when he plays the pipes or dances to a wild tune, addresses someone with a poem, or exhibits supernatural powers" (Schoon Eberly 63). But Peter II is a hybrid between a human and a god (cf. Schoon Eberly 60) and not a changeling, thus rendering his treatment useless. The juxtaposition of Peter II's innocence and the drastic description of his treatment evokes pity in the reader.

The next stage of Peter II's life in *The Child Thief* includes a fay creature, a moss man called Goll (cf. C.T. 63), who is living outside human civilisation in Goll's hill. In the woods, Peter II has to catch spiders and fight for better food against a wolf (cf. C.T. 77). The wolf becomes a symbol for the oppressor who will take everything from Peter II, if he does not fight and kill him. To learn to fight one's fears is a step towards maturity, something that never truly seems to happen to Peter II, at least not to his physique (cf. C.T. 209). Peter II evolves mentally after Goll has been killed by human men, whom Peter II has drawn to Goll's hill, after he disobeyed the moss man and tried to befriend the children of the village (cf. C.T. 89). That night, after he killed the wolf, Peter II cries. His "tears were for Goll, but they were also for himself, a six-year-old boy without a mother, or a friend, scared, hated, and turns into the first Lost Child.

In the moss man's deathscene we have, if not the first, yet one of the most graphic depictions of violence and torture which leaves little room to imagination (cf. C.T. 88). The explicit descriptions of Brom are insofar very unlike Barrie's description of violence, as that Barrie often leaves out the description completely or writes about it in such a matter that it neither seems bloody nor gory (cf. P.P. 45, 55, 81).This seems unnecessary, since *Peter Pan* was, at first, intended for adults and not for children (cf. J. Rose 5). At least *The Little White Bird*, which contained the original *Peter Pan* – then called *Peter and Wendy,* had been intended for adults (cf. B. 93, J. Rose 75). Brom emphasises the cruelty and intensifies the violence he found in *Peter Pan* to such a degree that *The Child Thief*, therefore, cannot pass as a children's book like *Peter Pan.*

After Goll's death, Peter II finds an entrance to Avalon by chance and meets Ginny Greenteeth (cf. C.T. 131-136). During their first encounter, she entrances him with her voice and lures him into her burrow (cf. C.T. 135-136), where something very disturbing happens:

> She straddled him, leaning forward, letting her hair drape across his face. She placed a warm hand on his stomach, running her fingers up his chest, pushing the wolf pelt aside. She bent over and sniffed his hair, her breasts sliding along his bare chest as she sniffed his face, down his neck, then pressed her cheek against his chest. He felt the hot wetness of her mouth on his nipple.
> Peter felt his loins stir. He saw the three sisters behind the woman, watching, their eyes wide, feverous, drool running shamelessly down their chins.
> "My, he is a firm one," whispered the first.
> "Rigid as a tent post," chimed in the second.
> "We will feed a long time on this one," added the third and all three giggled. (C.T. 136)

This scene is not only disturbing because the witch entices him, but also because Peter II seems to be unable to not react to it. Barrie's Peter Pan "panics and avoids the advances of the three female figures in Neverland" (Wilson 605), and he does not even understand the females' wishes concerning him (cf. P.P. 111). Gilead wrote about Peter Pan: "Free of mortality, sexuality, and social responsibility, Peter is imprisoned by his own inability to grow up" (285). Apart from the point of sexuality, this statement is also true of Brom's Peter Pan. Brom seems to allude with this scene to the "fin-de-siècle exploration of perilous beauty and forbidden objects of desire" (Wood 159), meaning that Barrie's peers wrote poems and painted pictures "celebrating the beauty and sensual appeal of boys, […] that in today's political climate would probably be subject to censorship as child-pornography" (Wood 159). Fimi writes that fairies often had a sexual side in theatre and literature (cf. 59-60). The scene between Peter and the witch mixes the paedophiliac tendencies of Barrie's times (cf. Wood 157-158), with a rape fantasy and the sensuality of drinking someone's blood, alike to the motif of the vampire. According to folklore, Vampires are related to witches (cf. Heitz 136, 138) and are said to suck their victim's blood from their nipples (cf. Heitz 72).The sucking of blood is often seen as a replacement for intercourse (cf. Winnubst 9) and vampires are often linked to sexual actions, as in Bram Stoker's *Dracula* (cf. Yu 147). It may seem far-fetched, but the connection between the witch stiffening Peter II's penis, sucking blood from his nipple and poisoning him by that (cf. C.T. 143), and the motif of the vampire with its sexualised bloodsucking and the infecting of the victim (cf. Winnubst 8, 9) is there. In *The Child Thief*, the witch's scene is the only scene in which Peter II has a distinct sexuality. Otherwise, no female besides Modron – his substitute mother – shows any interest in Peter II. Modron's interest in Peter II, though, is the motor behind most of his actions. She saves him from the poison of Ginny Greenteeth's teeth and binds him to herself, thus robbing him of his choices, which could be seen as another mistreatment of a minor (C.T. 144).

    Brom then again plays with the fact that Barrie created Peter half bird and half human: Modron says that Peter II must be "part bird" and Peter II answers: "Why, I'm a Peterbird" (C.T. 146). Peter and Peter II both crow or at least make animal noises when they are exulted (cf. P.P. 66, C.T. 35, 476). Peter II sacrifices everything in order to save Modron and with her Avalon, he even accepts the death of the children he brings through the Mist. The fact that he is the only one, who can walk through the Mist and bring the children to Avalon, is similar to Peter Pan's ability to take the Darling children to Neverland (cf. Fimi 37). Both Peter Pans take the children to a dangerous, magical place that might well be the place they die in. Peter is first introduced when Mrs Darling travels through the minds of her children and finds him especially often in Wendy's mind. And then she remembers that "there were odd stories about him; as that when children died he went part of the way with them, so that they should not be afraid" (P.P. 7-8). Gilead writes about Peter Pan that he empties the nursery "like aging and death" (286), when he fetches the Darling children. As mentioned before, this associates him with death, who accompanies souls to the afterlife, which could be the Neverland. Gilead writes that "forever young, he embodies the adult obsession with time and death" (285). She also states that "Neverland is the realm of death under the cover story of boyish fun and adventure" (Gilead 286). She links this statement to the fact that "the boys live underground, each in a house whose entrance fits him exactly, like a coffin" and that "Peter, like death, changes the boys to fit the entrances" (Gilead 286). The description of Peter as "lovely boy, clad in skeleton leaves and the juices that ooze out of trees" (P.P. 11) when he enters the nursery, leads Gilead to the deduction that "both boy eternal and rotting corpse, he arrives like a dream of immortality came true, but also like a plague deadly to children" (286). Still, the Lost Boys love him and obey his every order (cf. P.P. 62). It is the same in *The Child Thief*: Redbone is very fervent in his devotion to Peter II. He says: "I love that pointy-eared dude. He did more than save my life. He gave me a life. Gave me a family. I know what I'm about, 'cause it's all real simple here. We're clan. We're Devils and we look after one another", and Abraham and Dash agree with him (C.T. 162).

Peter Pan II is older than Peter Pan, who leaves the impression of a boy not older than ten years of age. Peter II wears "hand-stitched leather pants with pointy-toed boots sewn right into them" (C.T. 15). He has "a tangle of auburn, shoulder-length hair, a sprinkle of freckles across his nose and cheeks" and pointy ears (C.T. ix). His eyes are described to be gold like the eyes of a lynx (cf. C.T. ix). His exact height is not named, but we can assume that he has the height and build of a 14-15 year-old boy (cf. C.T. 15). Peter II also features some scars on his arms, brow, cheek and the neck (cf. C.T. 27). Nick, the Doubting Thomas among the Devils, thinks that "there was just something compelling about the boy, something that made Nick want to follow even against his better judgement" (C.T. 21), and that "Peter felt like a friend, [...] one you could count on to watch your back" (C.T 25). Peter has "keen senses alert for the dispirited and desperate, the abandoned and abused, for the lost child. Because lost children needed someone to trust, needed a friend, and Peter was good at making friends" (C.T. 56). It is again Tanngnost who gives the explanation to the reader: He thinks that Peter II is "ever the contradiction. [...] One moment a cold-hearted killer, the next a sentimental boy, always the eternal optimist despite a lifetime of tragedy. Of course, that's his glamour" (C.T. 239). The eternal optimism might stem from Barrie's Peter Pan insofar, as he always forgets meanness and is stunned by it when he encounters it again (P.P. 97). In general, Peter Pan does not evolve or change, because he forgets everything that happens as if it were totally unimportant to him. He sometimes even forgets that he killed someone (cf. P.P. 81, 177) and he forgets Wendy (cf. P.P. 178). Peter never changes, he is "entrapped in an eternal present without emotional or cognitive meaning" (Gilead 287).

Peter II forgets many of the children, too. He starts mourning them at one point, when he thinks that the Lady is dead (cf. C.T. 423), and stops as soon as he gains the knowledge that she is alive (cf. C.T. 425). In the end he tries to remember their names and he mourns all the children that have died for his cause: "The tears kept coming until a harsh sob shook his frame. He slumped against the turtle as tears for Sekeu, Abraham, Goll, his mother, Nick, and all the Devils that had died for him poured freely down his cheeks. He slid to the grass. The list was long, but Peter sat there, eyes clenched, arms tight about his knees, until he could name every one – every single one" (C.T. 475). Peter II develops during the book and thus shows the reader a strange mixture of adult scheming and childish ruthlessness. In *The Child Thief*, nearly thirty people die through the hands of Peter II or the Devils' (cf. C.T. ix, 19, 217, 218, 284, 287, 293, 348, 395, 397, 399, 452, 453, 468). There are other scenes of slaughter to find in this book (cf. C.T. 387-388), but the Devils do most of the killing. Peter II is convinced that a "soul simply has not lived until they've heard the screams of their dying enemies" (C.T. 267). He often tries to emphasise that nothing, even killing someone, is as morally reprehensible as it seems (cf. C.T. 20). Brom writes on his homepage that he wondered what Peter Pan would be like "if the violence and savagery were presented in grim stark reality" (bromart.com). He executes these thoughts within *The Child Thief* and describes the violence in a very graphic way. Brom also asked himself what Barrie has meant by writing that Peter thins the Lost Boys out (cf. C.T. 478), and gives the answer in *The Child Thief*: "Peter shoved the knife into Leroy's chest" (405). The reader, though slightly shocked, cannot be surprised at how Leroy's life ends. Leroy killed his father over a beer (cf. C.T. 378) and killed Sekeu for an even smaller reason (cf. C.T. 336-337) – he was only susceptible to Ulfger's manipulation because he was a disturbed and violent person (cf. C.T. 334). So he deserved to die for his actions according to the logic of the book. That Peter II does kill him, without remorse or feeling guilty, is still highly unsettling and prompts the reader to think about the other boys he has left in the Mist to die (cf. C.T. 40) and about the other unnamed children that have died for his cause.

Unlike Peter Pan, Peter II has more than one main foe within Avalon: Captain Samuel Carver and the Reverend on the side of the settlers and Ulfger and Ginny Greenteeth on the side of the fairies. Ulfger is a son of the Horned One like Peter II (cf. C.T. 465), but he is temperamentally the near opposite of Peter II: He thinks that Avalon needs "*order* and *discipline*" (C.T. 176 orig. emphasis). His probably also mixed heritage lets him grow up, unlike Peter II who stays "a miserable snot-nosed brat" (C.T. 209). Peter II's mixed blood, foremost the human part, keeps "puberty at bay" (C.T. 208). Peter II is delighted that he does not have to turn into "one of those horrible, hairy brutish men" (C.T. 109) like Ulfger. While Peter Pan II does not grow up because of his genes and the fact that Avalon lies outside of time, Barrie's Peter Pan stayed a child because Barrie does not want him to. Yes, Peter does not let himself be adopted by Mrs Darling, but it is more probable that Barrie did not want Peter to grow up. Jacqueline Rose states: "Suppose, therefore, that Peter Pan is a little boy who does not grow up, not because he doesn't want to, but because someone else prefers that he shouldn't. Suppose, therefore, that what is at stake in *Peter Pan* is the adult's desire for the child" (3) – "the child" meaning childhood in this case, something that was not only coveted by Barrie, but also by his generation.

Peter II and Ulfger have been enemies from the very day that Peter II set foot on Avalon (cf. C.T. 193-195). Ulfger wants the Flesh-eaters to leave Avalon, too, but his belief in what Avallach and his dead father want becomes twisted until he starts to fight against his own allies (cf. C.T. 322). Tanngnost says that "Ulfger does have honor – in many ways it is his greatest undoing. He's tied to what he believes is his duty, no matter how distorted that may have become" (C.T. 223). He seems to be the counterpart to the Reverend with his warped ideology. A character like Ulfger does not exist, or only to a small part in Tinker Bell in *Peter Pan* (cf. P.P. 49).

The characters of Peter Pan and Peter Pan II have, besides all the differences in appearance and behaviour, many similarities. Both show disturbing traits of character (cf. P.P. 118, C.T. 107). Brom states that "the idea of an immortal boy hanging about nursery windows and seducing children away from their families for the sake of his ego and to fight his enemies is at the very least *disturbing*" (bromart.com orig. emphasis). They both show threatening attributes that make the children beware of them (cf. P.P. 88, C.T. 19). Furthermore, both enjoy fighting and killing (P.P. 96, 122, 139): "The soldier let out a horrified wail and Peter's eyes *gleamed*. He liked the sound, craved it" (C.T. 217). And to both of them everything they do seems to be a game of some sort – they cannot stay serious for long (cf. C.T. 16, 197, P.P. 42).

Concluding one can say that both Peters have similar traits of character, but their major difference lies in two points: Firstly Peter II is not blocked out by his mother, he still has tender feelings for her and a replacement in Modron; Secondly Peter Pan II grows during the book, and after Avalon is destroyed, he is free of Modron's charm and starts to think for himself (cf. C.T. 476). Peter "forfeits his humanity to preserve his fantasy" (Hunter 70) and stays a child by rejecting the mother figure, while Peter II grows up and is not Modron's dependent son anymore.

3.2. Cernunnos, the Horned One

In Barrie's Peter Pan there is no Horned God, no leader uniting an army. There is no need. In Brom's *The Child Thief* on the other hand, the figure of Cernunnos, or the Horned One (cf. Bober 14), is a necessity. When the settlers arrived and started killing the fairies, Modron "called on the Great Horned One to come out of the forest and crush the men" (C.T. 251). Peter likens him to a "mighty oak" and describes him to have "eyes flaming beneath the Horned Helm" (C.T. 251). His accessories are a war drum, the Horned Helm, a banner, and the famous sword Caliburn (cf. C.T. 251), which can be identified as the legendary sword Excalibur. During the first battle with the settlers, the Horned One is killed by the settlers' cannon and muskets (cf. C.T. 252).

Brom, as with Avalon, researched the Horned One's background. He states that he based this figure on "the Great Horned God, a modern syncretic term used amongst Wiccan-influenced Neopagans, that unites numerous male nature gods out of such widely dispersed mythologies as the Celtic Cernunnos, Herne the Hunter […], Pashupati in Hindu and the Greek Pan" (C.T. 280). He names Cernunnos first, which indicates that this God was his major source of inspiration for the figure of the Horned One. The earliest evidence of the Horned God "appears in the palæolithic period […]. He is wrapped in a deer-skin and wears antlers on his head […]. The Romans record Cernunnos throughout Gaul, especially in that part where the palæolithic horned god existed" (Murray 237). This indicates that Cernunnos inherited the aspects of this horned god. Bober states that "the stag god is probably the result of anthropomorphization of an animal divinity whose origin is lost in the penumbra of Celtic past, in the nomadic, aniconic existence before their arrival in Western Europe and North Italy" (18). This would explain how Cernunnos, Herne the Hunter, Pashupati and the Greek Pan could be merged into a god called The Great Horned God that Brom mentions. This palæolithic horned god seems to have merged with other gods and then re-emerged as the stag god, later Cernunnos, thus owning a relationship to a Hindu and a Greek god. The stag god reappears in the Celtic La Tène culture and his usual cross-legged pose has been established (cf. Bober 19). Cernunnos, also called the Horned One (cf. Bober 14), was Pre-Roman and antedates the Roman conquest (cf. Bober 14). Yet, the Romans influenced the natives and the natives "seem to have come to isolate this forestial domain from Cernunnos" (Bober 40). Though, in *The Child Thief* we seem, in Peter's memories at least, to be still at the forestial stage of the development of Cernunnos (cf. C.T. 59, 216). Cernunnos is also associated with fertility "not merely in an abstract sense of flourishing nature, but also in a specific reference to human fecundity and generation" (Bober 18). Brom uses this aspect of fertility, and gives Peter Pan his human mother, who has been seduced by the Horned God. The fertility of Cernunnos is depicted not only as a fact, but also as an exaggerated prejudice: "Why I bet you crawl around on your hands and knees before him, naked and grunting like a pig. Then bare your ass to the forest beast" (C.T. 216). Barrie named his Peter Pan "after the Greek god who symbolized nature, paganism and the amoral world" (B. 62). In the Balkan regions, the Greek influence transformed Cernunnos into Pan (cf. Bober 40). This fact suited Brom perfectly, for he depicted Peter Pan as the son of Cernunnos in *The Child Thief*. Whether intentional or by chance, Brom plays with the legends around Cernunnos and other horned gods, especially since *the horned one*, in German *der Gehörnte*, has been a term for the devil for a long time, and Peter Pan's clan, the Lost Children, do not only call themselves the Devils from Deviltree (cf. C.T. 251), Peter Pan is also called "devil" (C.T. 396) by the settlers.

3.3. The Females in Peter's Life

Not only has Brom changed and emphasised traits of Peter's character, he also changed the way females, and especially which females, interact with Peter Pan. Therefore, I will now analyse and compare the females in Peter's life.

3.3.1. Wendy, Tinker Bell and Tiger Lily

Wendy is introduced by Barrie as a "tidy child" (P.P. 9) and seems to be in love with Peter Pan right from the beginning. Even though Wendy has seen Peter Pan only in her dreams up to that point, she must be thinking a lot about him, for when Mrs Darling walks through her children's minds and tidies them up, she finds Peter's name "scrawled all over" (P.P. 7) Wendy's mind. Wendy is a mixture between little girl and grown-up middle-class woman. "Now Wendy was every inch a woman, though there were not so many inches" (P.P. 27). She loves Peter like a woman loves a man, even though in a somewhat subdued manner. She wants to kiss him and wants to be kissed in return, but this endeavour fails partly due to a misunderstanding about the meaning of the words kiss and thimble (cf. P.P. 32). Mostly, the kissing is a disappointment for Wendy because when Peter kisses Wendy, Tinker Bell intercedes and pulls Wendy's hair clearly out of jealousy (cf. P.P. 32). Wendy settles, more or less willingly, into being a mother and thus fulfilling the perfect image of a mostly asexual middle-class woman. "While Tinker Bell indulges in attiring herself, presumably for the pleasure of Peter, [...] Wendy presides over the dinner as if she were mother of the boys. It would seem that the role envisioned for middle-class women is that of mother, evacuated of any sexuality – which, because it contaminates, is displaced onto the working class" (Wilson 605).

Barrie includes another social or even cultural class into *Peter Pan*: Aboriginal Americans. They come in form of the Piccaninny Tribe and especially the beautiful Tiger Lily. "She is the most beautiful of dusky Dianas and the belle of the Piccaninnies, coquettish, cold and amorous by turns" (P.P.56). Tiger Lily is also presented incapable of speaking correct English – she uses pronouns incorrectly and the word *very* turns into *velly* (cf. P.P. 106). "Through the figure of Tiger Lily, the stereotype of the over-sexed aboriginal figure is introduced. Like Tinker Bell, Tiger Lily desires Peter Pan. In an early manuscript that desire is articulated through a rape fantasy" (Wilson 606). The three women in *Peter Pan*, are all in love in some way with the boy that never grows up. Tinker Bell is representing the feisty, full-blooded, sensual woman of the working class. She is described as "exquisitely gowned in a skeleton leaf, cut low and square, through which her figure could be seen to the best advantage. She was slightly inclined to *embonpoint*" (P.P. 23-24). Tinker Bell is the only one who has a room to herself. She has a little recess in the wall of the home underground to herself. She can shut herself off by drawing a curtain which "Tink, who was most fastidious, always kept drawn when dressing or undressing" (P.P. 78). The fact that she withdraws from the other children shows her intensified sexuality compared to Wendy's low sexuality. Fairies were often depicted in Barrie's times as sexually active and sensual. A good example for the sensual way to depict fairies is an exhibition of Thomas Heatherley's pictures. When he painted, for example, the picture *Fairy Seated On A Mushroom* in 1860, the erotic contents of his pictures "were only sanctioned because of the distance afforded by their depiction of mythical beings rather than flesh-and-blood women" (Nicholson 209). In one scene, Barrie describes the fairies coming home "from an orgy" (P.P.75). Tinker Bell is perfectly featured, but she is very small and literally single minded: "Tink was not all bad: or, rather, she was all bad just now, but, on the other hand, sometimes she was all good. Fairies have to be one thing or the other, because being so small they unfortunately have room for one feeling only at a time [...]. At present she was full of jealousy of Wendy" (P.P. 49). Ann Wilson has analysed the three female figures in Peter Pan's non-existent love life. She states that "each of the three female figures attracted to Peter Pan recognizes the other's desire for him, even if he is oblivious. Tinker Bell reacts with obvious jealousy, pulling at Wendy's hair and, when Wendy is arriving in Neverland, telling the boys that Peter has ordered them to shoot her" (Wilson 604). This is a drastic measure, but Tinker Bell is either wholly good or completely bad, she has no room for second thoughts or for thoughts about the consequences of her actions. Wendy is very naïve in comparison to Tinker Bell. She follows Tinker Bell blindly into the trap. "She did not yet know that Tink hated her with the fierce hatred of a very woman" (P.P. 50). Through Wendy's naïvety and her natural good behaviour she is forced into the aforementioned asexual role of a mother for the lost boys.

After she has been shot, the Lost Boys build a house around her. It is a complete house with roof and chimney and enforces the connection of Wendy to the domestic life of a house-wife. Soon she fully commits to the make-believe to be the mother of the

Lost Boys and at some point Peter starts impersonating their father. Peter and Wendy turn into parents, mock-impersonating these figures of authority. The Lost Boys know that Peter is not their real father (cf. P.P. 107), but they play along. Wendy hardly falls out of her role as the caring, loving mother. She cooks the boys' meals (cf. P.P. 78), darns their socks, and sews new clothes for them (cf. P.P. 79). She behaves entirely like a mother, but she is still a "young mother" and does not really know what she is doing (P.P. 88). Contrary to her young age, Peter calls Wendy "old lady" (P.P. 109) while impersonating the father, but instead of acting like a man, or like a father, he answers her timid question "Peter [...] what are your exact feelings for me?" with "those of a devoted son, Wendy" (P.P. 111). She has motherly feelings for him, but not solely so. She also wants something else, which may not be spoken out openly, and Peter does not understand the allusions and stays absolutely clueless as to Wendy's or Tiger Lily's motives. "You are so queer [...] and Tiger Lily is just the same. There is something she wants to be to me, but she says it is not my mother" (P.P. 111). Wendy reacts angrily to Peter's puzzled answer (cf. P.P. 111). This anger has its source in her love for Peter which is not entirely a maternal love. In this respect, Wendy differs from Modron, the mother figure Brom gave to Peter Pan. She falls out of her role as mother by loving Peter. The refusal of Wendy's slightly sexual love, again, pushes Wendy into her motherly behaviour, however much it vexes her: "she was far too loyal a housewife to listen to any complaints against father. 'Father knows best,' she always said, whatever her private opinion must be" (P.P. 106).

Wendy's maternal side was Barrie's attempt at representing the perfect white woman with her "'natural' inclinations to maternity" (Wilson 608) and as a figure with the "virtues of English womanhood" (Wilson 608). While Wendy is presented in the best ways possible, Tiger Lily is stereotyped in a negative way that finds its expression also through her lesser command of English compared to Wendy (cf. Wilson 608). In earlier manuscripts, we find stronger presences of Tiger Lily, which "are horrific in their suggestion that aboriginal women so strongly desire white men that they want to be violently conquered through rape" (Wilson 607). According to Ann Wilson, this was obvious and at the same time embarrassing for the contemporary reader (cf. 607), for it played right into the stereotypical notions people had against aboriginal people, and they knew that these stereotypes were often falsely magnified prejudices.

Because of her polite reserve and yet great care for others, Wendy is being treated specially not only by the lost boys but also by the pirates:

> A different treatment was accorded to Wendy [...]. With ironical politeness Hook raised his hat to her, and offering her his arm, escorted her to the spot where the others were being gagged. He did it with such an air, he was so frightfully distingué, that she was too fascinated to cry out. She was only a little girl. (P.P. 129)

As long as Wendy is in charge of the situation, she assumes the role of a mother, but when the events spin out of control, Wendy resides to being a little, frightened girl and absolutely useless in the fight between the Lost Boys and Hook's pirates on the Jolly Roger. Tinker Bell, who represents the simple-minded working class, tries to change given situations by behaving naughtily and scheming against Wendy and thus assumes some kind of control over certain situations without thinking about the outcome. Wendy, as the embodiment of the perfect English woman on the other hand, does not usurp any power. She only uses the given status as mother and gives it up as passively as she assumed it. Tiger Lily plays only a small role in *Peter Pan*, and is highly stereotypical, which makes her a flat character without any change in her personality. On the one hand, Tinker Bell and Tiger Lily, who have their origin in the Neverland, do neither reflect upon their situation, nor do they evolve. They stay flat characters. Wendy on the other hand keeps some kind of distance. She "acknowledges the desirability of fantasy but also the need to reject it. She provides a constant standard of reality within Never Land which allows her to learn about herself" (Hunter 70). Wendy sometimes seems to be outside the system of Neverland. She differs from all the other figures of Peter Pan. When enacted on stage – Barrie wrote it as a play for the theatre after all – "Wendy is *Peter Pan's* ground, the voice of reason, the feminine, domestic site of stability and normalcy" (Wolf 506). The fact that she is the opposite of Peter Pan, Tinker Bell and the Lost Boys, that she thinks about herself and learns throughout the story allows her to grow up in the end and be also somewhat ashamed about it. She longs for the Neverland and wants to go back, yet accepts the course of time and allows Peter to leave with her daughter (cf. P.P. 182-184). Wendy stays in some ways a little child that wants to play with Peter and fly away with him, but now she really has become an adult and a real mother. Her feelings for Peter have become solely maternal and she has transformed into the perfect, English middle-class woman. Barrie epitomised in her, the "image of the substitute mother", as his mother had been to her little brother (B. 6).

3.3.2. Sekeu – Warlord or Mother?

Sekeu is a Native American and, though not explicitly expressed, we get the idea that she has been with Peter the longest of all Lost Children. Redbone states that "Sekeu has been here since the pilgrims. She was a slave of the Delaware tribe" (C.T. 158). It is Nick, the newest member of the Lost Children, who gives us the most detailed description of Sekeu.

> She had the wide cheekbones and a strong jawline of a Native American Indian. Her body was lean and sinewy. [...] as she neared, he noted the hard set of her face – especially the eyes, they didn't look like the eyes of a child [...]. Her copper-coloured skin was dirty and dotted with scars, leaving no doubt she'd seen her fair share of trouble. Her long black hair was captured in twin braids that ran down her back. Two black wings were threaded through a broad, beaded headband. The feathers swept downward from the sides of her head, the tips touching the tops of each shoulder, giving her a noble bearing. (C.T. 96)

This description is meticulously envisioned in Brom's paintings of Sekeu. He depicted her with little to no traits that we would consider female. She has hardly any breasts (C.T. 108) and does wear clothes made of leather and animal hides. She also wears a sword belted around her hips (C.T. 108), an item that is usually considered a masculine accessory. Silva states that "the military demands physically and mentally tough, goal-oriented, aggressive soldiers with skills of violence, weaponry and, ultimately, death" (937-938). Contrary to Barrie's Wendy, Sekeu has assimilated to the military setting and has become one of the fiercest warriors of the Devil Clan (C.T. 283, 285). Sekeu is neither naïve nor childlike. Her body is described and depicted as boyish and young, but she has lived several decades and is according to her real age an old lady. Sekeu knows what she is doing, yet she must have stayed somewhat adolescent in her thoughts, otherwise she would have become a Flesh-Eater. Contrary to Wendy, Sekeu is not forced into the role of a mother, she assumes it in the parts that suit her, but she refuses the parts that do not suit her. Sekeu is, like Wendy rather asexual. This asexuality stems from her position as a leader of the Devils, not from her role as mother for anyone. Sekeu does not flinch away from the thought to kill Nick, if he should become corrupted (C.T. 240). She shows a high level of coldness and determination. She might not be within the military, but the group of Devils is a military setting; the children being trained by Sekeu to become fighters (C.T. 113-115). "The social psychological perspective […] asserts that gendered behaviour is primarily the result of social and cultural determinants, being minimally influenced by physiological determination" (Bender-Slack 16). Moffatt and Norton fully agree with her, saying that especially children and newcomers learn how to perform gender from the community of practice or the discourse of gender they are culturally embedded in (106).

But a fighter is not all that Sekeu is or can be. She encourages the children (C.T. 96, 116), tries to strengthen their confidence (C.T. 115) and teaches them to be strong, to fight back, because otherwise they will "always be the brunt of brutes" (C.T. 114). Like Wendy, Sekeu supervises domestic activities: "She was busy refereeing breakfast and getting the fires going" (C.T. 152). She rubs ointment on their wounds (cf. C.T. 227), but treats them with a little more emotional distance than a mother would, though, especially towards the New Blood, who are not yet clan, not yet family to her (cf. C.T. 98). She says: "That is the problem with you runaways. You believe you can always run from your troubles" (C.T. 98). Sekeu voices her opinions without a doubt. Jaqueline Rose states that "when we speak, we take up a position of identity and certainty in language" (16). Sekeu's remark seems hypocritical considering the back-ground of her flight from slavery (C.T. 158). She must know how Nick feels, but she seems to have pushed all these memories away and elevated herself in some way above children like Nick. Her chiding can transform into judge- and punishment when she settles disputes between the children, who often fight amongst each other (C.T. 120), and when they behave inappropriately (C.T. 115) or even wrong (C.T 328). She acts like a parent in these cases, but not in a way that we would identify as motherly. Burns-Ardolino writes that "masculine displays indicate power and dominance, while feminine displays indicate submission and vulnerability" (44-45) and vice versa. Sekeu is neither submissive nor does she seem vulnerable. She acts like the chief of the clan of Devils. Redbone follows her orders, but mocks her at the same time: "He gave Sekeu a *sieg heil* salute and winked at Nick" (orig. emphasis C.T. 156). The reference to Hitler is an insinuation to an absolute power over the group, but Sekeu's leadership is in fact limited and not absolute. She cedes her power to Peter as soon as he is back: ""Peter," Sekeu whispered. "Do we run?"" (C.T. 202). It is also Peter, everybody turns to, when Sekeu is critically wounded (C.T. 298). He cries for her and risks everybody's lives in order to save her (C.T. 299 ff) – an action that ultimately fails, but shows the close connection that exists between Sekeu and Peter (C.T. 323). This is another difference between Wendy and Sekeu. Wendy loves Peter like a woman loves a man. There is no indication whatsoever that Sekeu loves Peter Pan other than as friend, saviour and leader.

Sekeu fully supports Peter's cause, yet she is more evenly tempered and seldom acts rashly. She is the often ignored voice of reason and caution of the group of Devils (cf. C.T. 207). She admonishes him to be cautious: ""This is madness. You must not go to Lady's Wood. Elves will kill you."" (C.T. 207). In her agitation, her accent increases and emphasises her ethnicity. Redbone plays with that image and also with Sekeu's sexuality. Contrary to Peter, who is about her age, and contrary to the Witch, who is female, Sekeu has hardly any link to sexuality. The only scene that has some sexual innuendo is the scene with Redbone, in which Sekeu immediately puts him in his place:

> Redbone came up behind Sekeu and jabbed her in the butt.
> "Squaw, paleface need'um pow wow."
> Sekeu spun around, leading with her fist. Redbone was ready for her and leaped back, but she caught him on the arm so hard that even Nick flinched. [...] "What do you want?" Sekeu snapped, looking ready to take his head off. (C.T. 152)

In this instance, Brom alludes to Sekeu's ethnicity and sexuality, traits that Barrie used to subliminally display gender and class differences. This one scene emphasises at first glance her femininity. At a second glance, her quick retribution and her anger at being reduced to a female, a lesser being, make her seem emancipated and more masculine. This action also redeems her in our eyes, because "people tend to admire women whose traits they define as somewhat masculine" (Jacobson Michaelson 252). According to Butler, a female body should be an instrumentality of the woman's freedom, not a "defining and limiting essence" (17). Burns-Ardolino remembers to have experienced feminine clothing and being female as "encumbrances that hindered and deterred" her (42). She states that the process of becoming a woman is a "habituated and routinized process, wherein it is the primary responsibility of mothers, aunts, teachers and other women who are role models to prepare, train and initiate a girl into womanhood" (Burns-Ardolino 42). We know that within the group of Devils there is no aunt or mother or role-model that could have taught Sekeu how to be more feminine. "It is accepted as a theory of how women are psychically 'induced' into femininity" (Rose J.28). This can only have taken place incompletely in Sekeu's case, for we cannot define her gender. Her feminine side can rather be defined by her position as centre of the group and her direct link to every Devil. For David Bakan femininity manifests itself in the sense of being at one with other organisms, in contact, openness and union, while masculinity has its manifestation in self-protection – a trait that Sekeu also shows –, self-assertion and self-expansion, meaning that masculinity shows itself in the urge to master and in the repression of thought, feeling and impulse (Bakan qtd. in Jacobson Michaelson 252).

Her death is equally ambivalent. On the one hand, she dies a warrior's death – by the sword – and on the other hand she dies the death of a mother – asleep in bed at home (C.T. 337). Behind this image are the "traditional cultural notions of women as nurturers and men as warriors" (Silva 940). Femininity and womanhood are strongly linked to the domestic life of a mother and housewife, while weapons belong to a male warrior. Sekeu performs different modes of gender, masculine and feminine ones. On the one hand she educates the children, trains them, keeps them in line and supervises the cooking like a mother, on the other hand she is a very skilled warrior and participates in the chaos that the Lost Children live in. She is as much an element of order and moderation, as she is an element of chaos and violence. Sekeu does not think about performing gender. As Burns-Ardolino describes another woman: "The performativity that results in the achievement of the aim to sit does not occur to her" (46). Sekeu does not perform masculinity because she feels masculine. It is our social construct of gender of what is masculine that marks her as masculine or feminine. She only does what she needs to do in order to survive, and if that means becoming a soldier she becomes a soldier.

Thus we can say that Sekeu's gender is female with strong masculine traits. This might be a confusing find at first, but it is still logical if we consider her upbringing and her situation within the group of devils. Butler cautions us to only accept "intelligible" genders that are conform "with recognizable standards" (22). Butler states: "if gender is the cultural meanings that the sexed body assumes, then a gender cannot be said to follow from a sex in any one way" (10). Just because a gender does not meet our culturally defined standards, it may still be logical and intelligible. We only have to stop seeing people as wrong that do not meet these standards.

3.3.3. Modron

The Celtic legend of Modron is very old. Her status as goddess in her own right can be derived from the Celtic tutelary goddesses, who "were connected to the earth, wells or forests, or the animals who frequent them" (Sjoestedt 18). The Celts worshipped gods who were bound to or represented nature in some way. Sjoestedt writes that "not only mounds and caves" – as we have exemplified in Tír na nÓc – "but also deep waters belong to the gods" (47). And Modron was primarily the Giodelic and Brythonic development from "an ancient Celtic divinity of the waters" according to Loomis (*Morgain* 199). Her name Modron is derived from the goddess Matrona (cf. Loomis *Combat* 68). Matrona was "widely worshipped from Cisalpine Gaul to the Rhine Valley and gave her name to the Marne and other rivers in Gaul" (Loomis *Combat* 68). Brom writes about Modron that he found her in Welsh mythology – a fact that Loomis confirms: "The oldest Welsh texts tell little of Modron, except […] that she was also the mother of Mabon" (Loomis *Morgain* 194). The fact that she is seldom named in Welsh folklore is due to the Christian belief. Though her name was often suppressed, "stories about her continued to circulate and to be firmly believed" (Loomis *Combat* 68). Modron is only mentioned in Welsh sources and, though being Christianised, the region of Wales was inhabited over some time by Celtic tribes – tribes that may have believed in tutelary goddesses, as we know them from Celtic Ireland. Modron seems to be a conglomerate of many beliefs. On the one hand we have tutelary goddesses living in rivers and wells and on the other hand we have a Gaulish goddess called Matrona, who is connected to rivers, too. But Modron is not only connected to rivers, she is rather connected to the element of water, even though "the association of Modron with a river-crossing is perhaps older than any other feature of her story" (Loomis *Combat* 68).

Modron's connection to the element of water in a wider sense stems from the tale of the lake Llyn y Fan Fach, in which a mortal man gains the affection of the fairy, clad in white – a feature that becomes important later – who resides within that lake and surfaces in order to comb her hair (cf. Rhys 3-8). She brings into the marriage herds of cattle, sheep and goats (cf. Rhys 8), which can be read as a sign of high fertility. Brom included the aspect of fertility and the white dress into his version of Modron, which is in many points an accurate account of the legends around her (cf. C.T. 141).

There are some key aspects to Modron: Being the daughter of Avallach, the wife of a mortal, Mabon's mother, living in a lake, wearing white, and being a goddess in her own right. Brom uses all these key aspects, but he changes some of them slightly, for example: she is still mourning her vanished son Mabon (cf. C.T. 187), when according to legend he had been found many years after his abduction. Also the depiction of her as a *barren* fertility goddess stems from Brom's imagination alone (cf. C.T. 141). In the Welsh legends she had one other son, Owain (cf. Loomis *Morgain* 199), and was not infertile after she gave birth to Mabon.

Mabon is, both in the legends and in Brom's *The Child Thief*, a major theme of Modron's story. Modron, who was bound to the lake in a slightly different story than the one told by Rhys, was found and coveted by Urien Rheged, a Christian. She says that "it is my destiny to wash here until I have a son by a Christian, and I am the daughter of the King of Annwn" (Loomis *Combat* 67). Urien begets Mabon by Modron. The legends all match insofar as that Mabon was abducted when he was only three days old (cf. Loomis *Morgain* 194). He was then imprisoned in Caer Loyw (cf. Sayers 20), a horrible prison (cf. Baudiš 54). When he is rescued, he is bewailing his fate, because "no one was ever so severely confined in prison before" ("The Triads No XV" 194). Mabon is found and returns to his mother, but in *The Child Thief* Mabon stays lost and Modron, in desperate search for a son and replacement for Mabon, adopts Peter and binds him to her person (cf. C.T. 141-144). In *The Child Thief*, Ginny Greenteeth hints at other boys who lost themselves in Modron's charm (cf. C.T. 141), but Peter ignores the witch because Modron compels him to follow her into the lake and beneath the water. There she binds him to her and heals his wounds (cf. C.T. 144).

Modron's background also includes the legend that she taught her oldest son how to use healing plants and, again, that she lived under a lake (cf. Whitehurst Williams 41) as in Rhys' retelling of the story of Llyn y Fan Fach, even though she is not mentioned by name. Loomis states: "Though we have little record of Modron under her own name [...] we have some compensation in the many folktales of a usually nameless fey that seems to have inherited the Modron tradition" (Loomis *Morgain* 195). Concerning Modron's abode, the lake, we know of at least one other distinctive fairy creature that resides within lakes and comes out to dance on the green: The White Lady (cf. Beck 295). The legends that have formed around so called White Ladies are insofar interesting, as that Brom seems to have included some of their qualities in his version of Modron. We have the connection of Modron to the apple via Avallach's apple tree as a symbol for fertility, and we have the story of Llyn y Fan Fach, where she brings herds of animals as dowry, which is also a sign of fertility (cf. Wilkie 202). The fact that Brom made the lake her abode connects her to the stories of the White Ladies which can in turn be identified as deities of "fertility and grain, which is closely related among Celtic and Teutonic peoples" (Beck 203). Nancy Arrowsmith lists the White Ladies as the northern equivalent of the southern Fate, Fées, Hadas and Korrigan, who are elves of fertility and growth, too (cf. 31). Brom clad his Modron in white, just as a White Lady would be clad in white. He also gave her white hair and white, nearly translucent skin (cf. C.T. 143). According to Jane Beck, White Ladies also wanted little boys to follow them. Beck quotes from a young boy's story, in which a White Lady promises him treasure, if he follows her. He says that she sat down on his bedside, "wrung her hands and cried sore", then kissed him and asked him to go with her (294). Even if the White Lady really wanted him to have the treasure in the aforementioned case, she is still charming a little boy away from his home to follow her to an unknown end. Contrary to that White Lady, Modron instantly assumes the role of a mother towards Peter and he instantly obeys and trusts her.

In Modron we have a clear mother-figure for Peter Pan, without any sexual content, even though she is considered by Ulfger to be fickle and frivolous (cf. C.T. 173). To Peter, she is only the mother, the mother of everything, everybody and especially him. She differs greatly from the Wendy that Barrie gave Peter for a substitute mother. Modron is neither human, nor does she have a stable character, she is selfish and does not think twice about the sacrifices that are made for her in order to reach her ultimate goal: the salvation of Avalon. At the end, when Avalon is destroyed and saved at the same time, she even wants Peter to leave everything behind, to follow her, and forget his promises to Nick (cf. C.T. 473).

3.4. The Lost Boys

The Lost Boys are Peter's constant companions and his subordinates. The mechanics in their group in comparison to the mechanics in the group of the Lost Children will be shortly analysed in the following.

3.4.1. Barrie's Lost Boys

The Lost Boys are, according to Peter, "children who fall out of their perambulators when the nurse is looking the other way" and "if they are not claimed in seven days they are sent far away to the Neverland to defray expenses" (P.P. 31).We cannot be sure whether they die after seven days and thus come to the Neverland, or whether they come to Neverland by magic. Barrie seems to leave this specific detail to the reader's imagination. The boys vary over time (cf. P.P. 52), but portrayed in *Peter Pan* are Nibs, Slightly, Curly, the Twins and Tootles (cf. P.P. 52-53). Together with the three Darling children and Peter there are nine Lost Boys plus Wendy, of whom we can safely say that she is not a boy and stands outside the group while still belonging to them. The Lost Boys even shoot Wendy because they think that Peter ordered them to and "it was not in their nature to question when Peter ordered" (P.P. 62). It is not surprising that they act this way, "given that they have been trained to obediently follow the orders of their Captain, they shoot arrows at her until she falls to earth, which Tootles believes will make Peter proud of him" (Wilson 603), but Peter's absolute control over the boys is, at times, disturbing, especially in the aforementioned case. Brom states that with the Lost Boys "Peter Pan has turned bloodletting into a sport, has taught them not only to kill without conscience or remorse but also to have a damn good time doing it" (bromart.com/childthief). This depiction is not unusual because "boys were increasingly represented as plucky and clever but also largely amoral and often cruel" (Deane 690).

The dynamics in this group are difficult to see and analyse. Wendy is the mother who is tender and mends that which is broken, she cooks the food and darns their socks (cf. P.P. 78). Peter is sometimes the father figure (cf. P.P. 106), but more often he is the leader in battle and play (cf. P.P. 88) which can be very similar in the make-believe world of the Neverland. The Lost Boys themselves are usually passive and either following Peter's lead or listening to Wendy and her orders as a mother (cf. P.P. 103). Even though the boys have different characters (cf. P.P. 52-53), they act together as a group. Tinker Bell, who is not a Lost Boy herself, adds a note of discord to the group with her sometimes selfish and ignorant behaviour (cf. P.P. 68). She seems to be the element of chaos, an element that can change the outcome of the story completely by seemingly random behaviour, but this behaviour can be identified as jealousy- and love-induced. Her jealousy turns Tinker Bell mischievous and meddlesome (cf. P.P. 52) and her love for Peter drives her to heroic deeds, for without Tinker Bell Peter would have died (cf. P.P. 136-137). Barrie's Lost Boys are a homogeneous group whose daily routine is not described in detail and the details are left for the reader to fill out with his or her imagination.

3.4.2. Brom's Lost Children

The Lost Children are very different from Barrie's Lost Boys. For instance, the group consists of boys and girls instead of only boys. In Barrie's times, the adventure novel was read by male readers, while the domestic story was for female readers (cf. J. Rose 77) – two genres that Barrie mixed with each other in Peter Pan – but the times have changed. The theory of intertextuality suggests that a text cannot be read as a singular work of art, but always has to be seen in the context it is produced in, so that "meaning becomes something which exists between a text and all the other texts to which it refers and relates" (Allen 1). In the case of the Lost Children in comparison to the Lost Boys, we have to count in the emancipation of the females. In our modern society, girls can be as strong and free as boys, and Brom reacts to this emancipation by filling the ranks of the Lost Boys with girls and transforming the part of Barrie's book which directly spoke to boys and their hunger for adventures into a multi-gendered group that includes boys as well as girls. Sekeu, for example, has a high rank in the pecking order of the Lost Children. The word pecking order is in this case closer to the reality in which these children live than the word hierarchy. Sekeu describes them as "the lost, the wild, the untamable[sic]" (C.T. 96). They call themselves "Devils" (C.T. 96) and see themselves as a clan, "the children of the wolf mask" (C.T. 96). Sekeu has been with Peter for a long time and has become one of his closest friends (cf. C.T. 323).

She has some authority over the children (cf. C.T. 327) which stems from her long years at Peter's side and her fighting experience. In the group of children we have a far more complex net of social relations and interactions than in Barrie's group of Lost Boys. The Devils are, for instance, split into two distinct groups: the Devils and New Blood.

In order to become a Devil, a part of the clan, the child in question has to pass three tests. The first test is the transition of the Mist, which Nick, who is essential for our view on the Lost Children, passes well (cf. C.T. 46) according to Peter. The second test is a kind of initiation rite, in which he has to master his fear and show his mental strength by not giving up and fighting back (cf. C.T. 69-72). After this test he is proclaimed "New Blood for Deviltree" (C.T. 73). In this scene, the Devils are depicted as barely human, "their bodies gangly and spidery" (C.T. 69). They are adorned with hides, bones, tusks and twigs, feathers and antlers (cf. C.T. 70).The third and final test is shedding the blood of an enemy in order to "enter the ranks of Devil Kind" (C.T. 110), until that point the children are categorised as "unproven" (C.T. 110). Through Nick, the reader has an insight into the finer mechanics of the divided group, a feature that does not originate in Barrie's *Peter Pan*. Nick tries to distance himself from the group mentally. He seems to voice Brom's thoughts about the Lost Children. Brom wonders how children would really "react to being kidnapped and thrust into such a situation" and how hard it would be for them "to fall under the spell of a charismatic sociopath, to shuck of the morality of civilization and become cold-blooded killers" (bromart.com/childthief). Nick thinks about what is happening around him and in some ways he fights it. He does not succumb so easily to Peter's charms. It takes Nick a long time, but when he finally has found his own cause to fight, he thinks "*I've totally lost my mind. And it was amazing how good it felt*" (C.T. 268, orig. emphasis). On his first meeting with Peter "Nick wasn't sure if he was thrilled or terrified" (C.T. 18). This theme is repeatedly picked up by Brom in Nick's thoughts, yet he sometimes seems to be unable to help himself around Peter, and still goes along with what Peter suggests (cf. C.T. 26, 31, 34), partly because Peter knows what Nick needs: a friend.

Nick has been abused by Marko, the tenant of his mother, and has fled his home (cf. C.T. 4). This way, he became a lost child. He realises over time that his mother acted out of need, and the love he still feels for his mother helps him fend off the charm of Modron (cf. C.T. 326). His antagonism towards Peter earns him the hostility of the other Devils. While Redbone knocks him violently down to earth (cf. C.T. 161), Sekeu reacts sternly, but more rationally and understanding (cf. C.T. 97). Like Wendy, she is the often ignored voice of reason and caution of the group of Devils (cf. C.T. 207). Both, Sekeu's as much as Nick's advice are ignored, especially regarding the Flesh-eaters. Nick is the only one who points out to Peter where the flaws in Peter's logic lie, but he does not listen (cf. C.T. 368, 406). Contrary to Peter, Nick understands his own flaw. He understands that leaving his mother was the wrong choice. He ran away instead of fighting against Marko and helping his mother (cf. C.T. 231). Nick learns that he has to fight against his opponents, if he does not want to lose everything.

This brings us to the subject of violence within the group of Devils. The violence and enmity between Leroy and Nick is something that does not exist between Barrie's Lost Boys. One might argue now that Tootles shot Wendy, but Wendy was not yet a part of the group, the way Nick is. The violence usually originates from Leroy and is directed at the other unproven children, especially at Nick because he is strong and learns to fight back (cf. C.T. 111), just as Sekeu advises him to (cf. C.T. 114). Leroy is a general problem within the structure of the Devils, for he sees Nick as a danger to his status and threatens him repeatedly (cf. C.T 112). He is liar and a coward, but Peter does not see the difference between a Lost Child, that has been abused and is therefore ready to fight against everyone and everything, and in desperate need of a friend like Nick, and a Lost Child that is simply violent, disturbed and mentally sick like Leroy (cf. C.T. 378). This might be the major difference between Barrie's Lost Boys and Brom's Lost Children: the Lost Children have not simply gone lost because they fell out of their perambulators. The Lost Children decide to embrace a life for which they have to fight and eventually die because they prefer the life within the clan and a place to stay to a life of physical and mental abuse (C.T. 255). The Lost Children form a social group that is "defined not primarily by a set of shared attributes, but by a sense of identity" (Sedinger 40). This identity is the identity of an abused child. Barrie's Lost Boys cannot remember their parents, or their mothers, while Brom's Lost Children actively try to forget their former lives, which makes all the difference.

3.5. The Pirates

The analysis of the group of pirates is maybe the most interesting, for Brom exchanged Barrie's Pirates with settlers, thus creating different opponents for Peter Pan.

3.5.1. Barrie's Pirates

In Barrie's work, the main antagonist of Peter Pan is Captain Hook. Barrie disguised himself sometimes as a pirate while playing with Silvia's children. His character's name was "Captain Swarthy, a dark and sinister figure who displayed a despicable cowardice in the face of his young antagonists, frequently forcing the four-year-old Peter to walk the plank into the murky waters of Black Lake" (B. 84). It seems to come natural to boys to want to play-fight. Deane cites Herbert Spencer, who claimed that "'the sports of boys, chasing one another, wrestling, taking prisoners […] gratify in a partial way the predatory instincts. No matter what the game, the satisfaction is in achieving victory, in getting the better of an antagonist'" (qtd. in Deane 692) and adds that this "valorization of play" was valued for its own pleasures and seen as a natural activity (Deane 692). Deane also states that the pirate was, in the Victorian imagination, strongly linked to boyhood and that books like *Treasure Island* were aimed both at men and boys (cf. 693). Whether Barrie fashioned Hook after Captain Swarthy or not is unknown, but he might have created Hook as a Neverland-version of Mr Darling "who escapes the pressures of being an adult by donning the guise of Captain Hook, a dandy – leisured and effeminate – who has the time […] to indulge in play and is free of the necessity to work" (Wilson 602). Thus Hook can be read as an escapist fantasy for adult, working men. In the case of Mr Darling, who is educated, it would explain Hooks high education, which is unusual for a man in his "calling" (Park Williams 485) and distances him from his crew.

In general, the depiction of the pirates in Barrie's *Peter Pan* is stereotypical for pirates. When they sing, they always sing the same song:

> Avast belay, yo ho, heave to,
> A-pirating we go,
> And if we're parted by a shot
> We're sure to meet below! (P.P. 53)

They are described as "villainous-looking" (P.P. 53) and to each of them Barrie has given an unimportant but fear-inducing physical trait or a bit of background-story like the story of "Cecco, who cut his name in letters of blood on the back of the governor of the prison at Gao" (P.P. 54) or the hands of Noodles, which are "fixed on backwards" (P.P. 54). Yet, in their midst, Captain Hook is described as the "blackest and largest in that dark setting" (P.P. 54). In contrast to Hook's crew Barrie describes him in detail. Hook is "never more sinister" than when he is "most polite" and fears the sight of his blood, "which was thick and of an unusual colour" (P.P. 55), a fact that Brom used in *The Child Thief*. Barrie writes: "This inscrutable man never felt more alone than when surrounded by his dogs. They were socially so inferior to him" (P.P. 141). Park Williams sees this again as a satire on men "being treated like dogs" and states that it "comes out in the Darling nursery, where, conversely, the dog Nana is treated like a human being" (485). On the one hand, this shows how evil pirates are, and how good, on the other hand, the Darling family is. The Pirate was "'reduced to a criminal pure and simple, the very negation of imperial social order'" (qtd. in Deane 694). This is not only true for the Victorian times, the pirate has been "'highly ideological from antiquity forward, functioning more or less as the maritime equivalent of barbarian'" (qtd. in Deane 694). Hook refutes this argument by being highly educated and elevated from his men. He is not even wholly evil (cf. P.P. 133), though his thoughts are formed in "the subterranean caverns of his mind" (P.P. 131), and he is not a barbarian; he treats Wendy like a gentleman would treat a lady (cf. P.P. 129). Hook has a soft moment in which he confides to his bosun Smee the story of his life (cf. P.P 59). This leads to Smee reminding him of Peter Pan, who cut off his arm and flung it to a crocodile "that happened to be passing by" (P.P. 60). Hook wants to kill Peter Pan for giving this crocodile a taste for him (cf. P.P. 60) and thus a reason to search Hook out. As a side note, Park Williams often stresses that Captain Hook and Captain Ahab show similarities: They both lost limbs to "seagoing monsters" (Park Williams 486), both show a "murderous red flashing of the eyes" (Park Williams 484) and "Moby Dick and Peter Pan are each the subject of unbelievably malign hatred" (Park Williams 487). This "malign hatred" is likened by Park Williams to the hatred a demon has for a god (cf. 487), and thus interprets Moby Dick, the Crocodile and Peter Pan as gods (cf. 486). When Peter finally vanquishes Hook in battle, he shows "bad form" (P.P. 160) and, satisfied, Hook decides to jump down into the sea, not knowing that the crocodile is waiting there for him (cf. P.P.160). This action seems atypical for Hook, but as Gilead states: "Hook is a comic-melancholy and murderously resentful adult obsessed with Peter, the pristine image of childhood and the past: envied, desired, and hated" (286). The fact that this pristine child shows bad form is enough to let Hook give up the fight and die. "In symmetrical fashion Peter hates Hook, the adult who seems to the child to embody the facts of generation, time, and mortality. Not surprisingly, Pan slays Hook only to become him" (Gilead 287).

3.5.2. Brom's Settlers

The Settlers in *The Child Thief* are no Pirates as in Barrie's *Peter Pan*. They happen to land on Avalon's shores, while thinking they have reached America (cf. C.T. 249). They eat not only meat, they also eat the magical creatures and are therefore given the name Flesh-eaters (cf. C.T. 253). Peter explains their twisted features with the loss of magic due to the "fear and hatred they harbor for all that they can't explain, control or understand" (C.T. 154). Their blood has turned black (cf. C.T. 353) and their skin has become scaly (cf. C.T. 391). They have no idea of what happens when Modron releases the Mist again and entraps them on Avalon, but they learn from a child they have captured that the Mist will evaporate when Modron dies and they will be able to leave Avalon (cf. C.T. 354). That is the reason why they have become "obsessed with clearing the whole island" of magical creatures and plants alike (C.T. 253). Through dialogues with each other we get to know the settlers first-hand as humans. They are sad, they have longings and they are not through and through bad people. They are rather people at the wrong place at the wrong time (cf. C.T. 390). Neither side, except for Nick, who notices the tragic irony of the whole situation, understands that both sides only want the settlers to leave the island of Avalon (cf. C.T. 368). Nick also sees them as humans:

> Somehow seeing their humanity made them all the more ghastly. Some horrible disease had infested their very core. Their skin was scaly, shriveled [sic], and black like that of a burn victim, and their faces were distorted as though in great pain. Their bodies were emaciated, their ribs and hips jutted out in sharp contrast to their shriveled [sic] waists. (C.T. 281)

Brom created, on the one hand, a totally different kind of enemy for Peter Pan: The settlers are no pirates, they are neither exceptionally virtuous, nor exceptionally evil. The only real danger is the Reverend in his fanaticism and his followers, who take the war against Avalon from a physical level to a metaphysical level as a war of the Christian god against the devil (cf. C.T. 446-448). The Reverend is Peter Pan's real enemy, the driving force on the settlers' side for warring on the magical creatures. The Reverend knows no mercy and even the Captain describes him as a "murderous madman" (C.T. 435) and hopes that "God be merciful, because these twisted men will not" (C.T. 364).

On the other hand, we can find in the Captain, whose name is Captain Samuel Carver – Carver being a play of words with Barrie's original Captain Hook – a tolerably well-educated man, not unlike Hook, who does not participate in the frenzy of the Reverend. He pities the Devils and sees, underneath all their paint and scars the children they are (cf. C.T. 354). He does not see any demons in the children as the Reverend does (cf. C.T. 370) and only participates in the public torture of the imprisoned Devils because he has to in order to survive (cf. C.T. 369). He has committed sins in his life before landing in Avalon, such as sleeping with "four wenches in Portugal [...] three being sisters and the last their mother", stealing a "basket of communion wine from the monastery" and taking the Lord's name in vain as many times as there were stars in the sky" (C.T. 358-359). Yet, in his heart he is a good man whose only wish is to know where the Lady "and her god-damned apple tree" are hidden, so he and with him all the settlers can leave Avalon (C.T. 358). He hates the options this decision leaves him with, because his way to Modron leads through the Lost Children and Peter Pan. He has less understanding for Peter than for the children whom Peter has kidnapped. The Captain says: "But mark my words, I shall make a trophy of his head yet" (C.T. 54). The Captain tries to show the children a way out, explains his side of the whole situation in order to win them over (cf. C.T. 361) but they love Peter too deeply to betray him, except for Danny (cf. C.T. 363). The Captain tries to save him later from the hands of the Reverend (cf. C.T. 435). The Captain has had sons and a wife, and becomes protective of Danny. He becomes heartsick when Danny embraces him, like his sons have done and decides to do everything to save Danny, even if it means to kill the Reverend and his minions (cf. C.T. 373). The Captain and the Reverend are enemies in their own rights and are constantly at war. The Reverend tries to isolate the Captain and gain total control over the settlers (cf. C.T. 399), and the Captain tries to keep his men safe from the Reverend while failing at it because the Reverend has become too powerful in all those years the settlers have stayed on Avalon. Contrary to Barrie, Brom created the enemies of Peter Pan from normal people who got corrupted. He gave them an understandable reason for their often indisputably horrible behaviour: the very human wish to be healthy and free. They are not evil out of sheer lust to kill Peter Pan like Barrie's Captain Hook.

4. Conclusion

Barrie's *Peter Pan* and Brom's *The Child Thief* have a few similarities, such as Peter Pan's need for a mother, or for friends, or his lust for killing. The two books are more different than alike, though. This is partly due to the intertextuality of the two books. "Peter Pan might mirror Barrie's personal […] dilemmas, but it also mirrored the taste of the Edwardian public, and in particular the prevalent cult of the child" (Avery 221). While Barrie's book is a mixture between a traditional fantasy and a modern fantasy, with elements of magic and strange characters and thematises "good versus evil and right versus wrong" (Kurkjian 494), *The Child Thief* seems to be a modern fantasy: detailed setting and credible characters that grow and change (cf. Kurkjian 494). Barrie's book has one time frame and one third-person narrator who uses clear-cut imagery for good and evil, while Brom's book has two time frames, a third-person narrator who takes the view of more than two characters, and ethics play a much greater role in *The Child Thief* than in *Peter Pan*. Barrie's third-person narrator leaves much to the imagination of the reader, especially concerning the violence. Brom states: "I simply love monsters, love the macabre, it is my youth, it is who I am, […] it is how I satiate my inner demons" (Bricken io9.com) and he lives up to this quote by describing not only violence and death, but by giving every figure he describes closely a feature that makes it disturbing and less good or less evil. Maybe the reason for his style lies in his wish to shock and unsettle the reader and make the reader rethink the original *Peter Pan*.

The future prospect of both Peters is different, too. Barrie's Peter Pan might go on like this forever, "so long as children are gay and innocent and heartless" (P.P. 185). Brom leaves the future of Peter Pan more open. He is has grown and changed, has become independent of Modron, is therefore able to fulfil the promises he made to Nick (cf. C.T. 474) and to mourn all the children he has led to their deaths (cf. C.T. 475). Brom's book can be seen as the third type of fantasy that Gilead describes: "the return neither normalizes fantasy as socializing therapy nor rejects fantasy as fostering a neurotic avoidance of social and psychic realities" (278). These differences raise the question, if Brom's *The Child Thief* is a retelling of Barrie's story in a time that would not accept the original *Peter Pan* the way it was accepted when Barrie wrote it. Barrie's original is a children's classic and therefore often read and beloved today, but we have to ask ourselves, whether Barrie would not have written *Peter Pan* today more like Brom wrote *The Child Thief* because it is decidedly more to the taste of the contemporary reader. It is important to include the theory of intertextuality in these thoughts, "since the text not only sets going a plurality of meanings but is also woven out of numerous discourses and spun from already existent meaning" (Allen 65). Hutcheon states that "the act of adaptation always involves both (re-)interpretation and then (re-)creation" (8). Therefore, Barrie's and Brom's books are as much a product of their minds as they are a product of the society they were written in (cf. Hutcheon 142). Further inquiry into these two books could yield answers to the question, whether Peter Pan can be seen as death in Brom's as well as in Barrie's version of the story. It is also quite interesting to research Peter Pan as a trickster god, who, like Loki in the Edda (cf. Von Schnurbein 115), changes sides (cf. P.P. 82), impersonates other figures (cf. P.P. 89, 150) and, though being cherished by both (cf. C.T. 162, 280), either goes against the gods (cf. C.T. 138, 221-223) or men-kind (cf. C.T. 287).

Concluding one can say that Brom answered his own question "what this children's book would be like […] if the violence and savagery were presented in grim stark reality" (bromart.com) with a book full of bloodshed and murder, whose causes lie in an even more disturbing set of abuse and violence.

5. Bibliography

Allen, Graham. *Intertextuality*. 2nd ed. London and New York: Routledge, 2011.

Anonymous. "The Triads No XV". The Cambo Briton 2 No 17 (1821): 193-196.

Arrowsmith, Nancy. *Das Große Buch der Naturgeister*. Trans. Michael Korth. Germany: Weitbrecht, (2000).

Atsma, Aaron J. *Hypnos*. http://www.theoi.com/Daimon/Hypnos.html. Accessed on 20th January 2014.

Atsma, Aaron J. *Thanatos*. http://www.theoi.com/Daimon/Thanatos.html Accessed on 20th January 2014.

Avery, Gillian. "The Quest for Fairyland." The Quarterly Journal of the Library of Congress 38 No 4 (1981): 220-227.

Barrie, James Matthew. *Peter Pan*. London: Penguin Classics, 1995.

Baudiš, Josef. "Mabinogion." *Folklore* 27 No 1 (1916): 31-68.

Beck, Jane C. "The White Lady of Great Britain and Ireland." *Folklore* 81 No 4 (1970): 292-306.

Bender-Slack, Delane. "The Role of Gender in Making Meaning of Texts: Bodies, Discourses and Ways of Reading." *Feminist Teacher* 20 NO 1 (2009): 15-27.

Birkin, Andrew. *J. M. Barrie and the Lost Boys – The Real Story Behind Peter Pan*. Second Printing. USA: Yale University Press (2005).

Bober, Phyllis Fray. "Cernunnos: Origin and Transformation of a Celtic Divinity." *American Journal of Archaeology* 55 No 1 (1951): 13-51.

Bricken, Rob. "*Our exclusive interview with legendary fantasy artist Brom!*" http://io9.com/our-exclusive-interview-with-legendary-fantasy-artist-b-1183378869. Accessed on 17th January 2014

Briggs, Katherine M. A *Dictionary of British Folk-Tales in the English Language Part B: Folk Legends*. Kindle Edition. 2013.

Brom. *The Child Thief.* USA: Harper Voyager, 2010.

Brom. www.bromart.com/childthief.html. Accessed on 13th January 2014.

Brom. www.bromart.com/bio.html. Accessed on 8th February 2014.

Burns-Ardolino, Wendy A. "Reading Woman – Displacing the Foundations of Femininity." *Hypatia* 18 No 3 (2003): 42-59.

Butler, Judith. *Gender Trouble – Feminism and the Subversion of Identity.* USA: Routledge, 1999.

Deane, Bradley. "Imperial Boyhood: Piracy and the Play Ethic." *Victorian Studies* 53 No 4 (2011): 689-714.

Evslin, Bernard. *The Adventures of Ulysses.* USA: Scholastic INC, 1969.

Fimi, Dimitra. *Tolkien, Race and Cultural History – From Fairies to Hobbits.* United Kingdom: Palgrave Macmillan, 2009.

Gilead, Sarah. "Magic Abjured: Closure in Children's Fantasy Fiction." *PMLA* 106 No 2 (1991): 277-293.

Heitz, Markus. *Vampire! Vampire! – Alles Über Blutsauger.* München und Zürich: Piper Verlag, 2008.

Hunter, Lynette. "J.M. Barrie's Islands of Fantasy." *Modern Drama* 23 No 1 (1980): 65-74.

Hutcheon, Linda and Siobhan O'Flynn. *A Theory of Adaption.* 2nd ed. London and New York: Routledge, 2013.

Internet Movie Data Base. http://www.imdb.com/name/nm1044909. Accessed on 8th February 2014.

Jakobson Michaelson, Evalyn, Leigh M. Aaland. "Masculinity, Femininity and Androgyny." *Ethos* 4 No 2 (1976): 251-270. Web.

Johnson, Judith E. "Women and Vampires: Nightmare or Utopia?" *The Kenyon Review* 15 No 1 (1993): 72-80.

Le Roux, Francoise and Christian-J. Guyonvarc'h. *Die Hohen Feste der Kelten*. Transl. Mag. Christian Schweiger. Göttingen: Arun-Verlag.

Krappe, A.H. "Avallon". *Speculum* 18 No 3 (1943): 303-322.

Kurkjian, Catherine, et al. "Children's Books: Worlds of Fantasy." *The Reading Teacher* 59 No 5 (2006): 492 – 503.

Lesnik-Oberstein, Karín. "The Psychopathology of Everyday Children's Literature Criticism." *Cultural Critique* 45 (2000): 222-242.

Loomis, Roger Sherman. "The Combat at the Ford in the 'Didot Perceval'." *Modern Philology* 43 No 1 (1945): 63-71.

Loomis, Roger Sherman. "Morgain La Fee and the Celtic Goddesses." *Speculum* 20 No 2 (1945): 183-203.

Moffat, Lyndsay and Bonny Norton. "Reading Gender Relations and Sexuality: Preteens Speak Out." *Canadian Journal of Education* 31 No 1 (2008): 102-123.

Murray, M.A. "269. The Horned God." *Man* 32 (1932): 237-238.

Nicholson, Helen. "Postmodern Fairies." *History Workshop Journal* 46 (1998): 205-212.

Park Williams, David. "Hook and Ahab: Barrie's Strange Satire on Melville." *PMLA* 80 No 5 (1965): 483-488.

Peyton III, Henry H. "The Myth of King Arthur's Immortality." *Interpretations* 5 No 1 (1973): 55-71.

Rhys, Sir John. *Celtic Folklore: Welsh and Manx, Volume 1*.[n.p., n.y.] Reprint by Bertrams Print on Demand, 2010.

Rose, Herbert Jennings. *Griechische Mythologie – Ein Handbuch*. Transl. Dr. Anna Elisabeth Berve-Glauning. München: C.H. Beck Verlag.

Rose, Jaqueline. *The Case of Peter Pan or the Imposibility of Children's Fiction*. USA: University of Pennsilvania Press, 1993.

Sayers, William. "'La Joie de la Cort' (Érec et Énide), Mabon, and Early Irish 'Síd' [Peace; Otherworld]." *Arthuriana* 17 No 2 (2007): 10-27.

Schoon Eberly, Susan. "Fairies and the Folklore of Disability: Changelings, Hybrids and the Solitary Fairy." *Folklore* 99 No 1 (1988): 58-77.

Shaw, Bernard. "Barrie: The Man with Hel in His Soul." *Shaw* 13 (1993): 151-153.

Silva, Jennifer M. "A New Generation of Women? How Female ROTC Cadets Negotiate the Tension between Masculine Military Culture and Traditional Femininity." *Social Forces* 87 No 2: 973-960.

Sjoestedt, Marie-Louise. *Celtic Gods and Heroes*. Mineola: Dover Publications (2000).

Von Schnurbein, Stefanie. "The Function of Loki in Snorri Sturluson's 'Edda'." *History of Religions* 40 No 2 (2000): 109-124.

Whitehurst Williams, Edith. "Morgan La Fee as Trickster in 'Sir Gawain and the Green Knight'." *Folklore* 96 No 1 (1985): 38-56.

Wilkie, E.M. *Legendary Stories of Wales*. USA: Pook Press (n.y).

Wilson, Ann. "Hauntings: Anxiety, Technology, and Gender in Peter Pan." *Modern Drama* 43 No 4 (2000): 595-610.

Winnubst, Shannon. "Vampires, Anxieties, and Dreams: Race and Sex in the Contemporary United States." *Hypatia* 18 No 3 (2003): 1-20.

Wolf, Stacy. "'Never Gonna Be a Man / Catch Me IF You Can / I Won't Grow Up': A Lesbian Account of Mary Martin as Peter Pan." *Theatre Journal* 49 No 4 (1997): 493-509.

Wood, Naomi. "Creating the Sensual Child: Paterian Aesthetics, Pederasty, and Oscar Wilde's Fairy Tales." *Marvels & Tales* 16 No 2 (2002): 156-170.

Yu, Eric Kwan-Wai. "Productive Fear: Labor, Sexuality, and Mimicry in Bram Stoker's *Dracula*." *Texas Studies in Literature and Language* 48 No 2 (2006): 145-170.